THE TEARS
THAT LINGER

THE TEARS
THAT LINGER

FROM THE HEART OF A FOSTER CHILD
BECAUSE THAT'S WHERE IT HURT
FROM THE MOUTH OF A
FOSTER PARENT BECAUSE I CARE

mary webb

To order additional copies of this book, contact:
Xlibris Corporation
1-888-795-4274
www.Xlibris.com
Orders@Xlibris.com
38877

CONTENTS

TRAIN UP A CHILD IN THE WAY HE SHOULD GO, AND
WHEN HE IS OLD HE WILL NOT DEPART FROM IT
PROVERBS 22:6

INTRODUCTION

This book was not put together to throw stones at anyone, or to deliberately hurt anyone. In this book each time that the word society is used it refers to the people that has made the decisions to make others lives miserable including children. We are referring to the genius that seem to think that a child should never be spanked at all, and under no circumstances yet one signature and the school can spank and whip as long as you tell them, the ones that lock up dead beat dads as they call them and let dead beat moms go free with next to no consequences, the ones that let a parent have parental rights that have told the system to take their kids and shove them, the ones that will pay a stranger a little money to take care of children and want the grand parents and relatives to do it for free. These are the ones referred to as society. The ones that make up the rules and they themselves break them at their convenience. You see just about everyone have a comment under cover. So what I did was gather up the information and put it in writing. I do not apologize for anything that is said in this book. I do hope and pray that it will in some way make a difference in the way laws and rules are put into place. Sometimes you might say that whoever derived these rules and standards could not have had children, and if they do oh well. So as you read this book do realize that this is information gathered from actual human beings, people that are really concerned and angry but will not come forward.

Some of the people that find these things bothersome are, yes, caseworkers, foster parents, children, plain workers and everyday people. A lot of the people that don't find anything wrong here are the ones that don't have a clue as to how the system works when dealing with this topic. So fasten your seat belt and let's ride.

Proverbs 22:6

Train up a child in the way he should go: and when he is old, he will not depart from it

One might ask the question—Does anyone really care?—Does anyone really understand? These are questions that are asked in reference to many aspects of life, not only foster care. When thinking on children that are in care and or children that have been adopted, even children in general these are questions that come up on a day to day basis. No, not in every child's life but in so many children's lives. When I think about it I often wonder if I have ever made a difference in a child's life, I would have to say, yes. Children that were in care—did I make a difference? I would have to say yes, again. Now, that they are gone, I miss them more than anyone could ever know. I hear from some of the children that I provided for periodically, and it's a joy to know that I am not forgotten, and to let them know that neither are they. Have you ever wondered how these children must think? Or, what they think? How they must feel? I did many times. Many many times I tried to put myself in the child's place, because I would watch the hurt that they would experience each time one of the children was removed from a place that they enjoyed being at or placed some place else. When thinking about the hurt that a child suffer, caused by being in this position, I thought to myself if I were a child in care would I think about some of the things they might think about such as running away ? Maybe! Being extra mean to the foster parent? Hate people for the rest of my life for the situation I was in? Yes, I probably would and really none of these things would do any good. I would think that for the most part most children that are in care think these are things that would really make a big difference. Possibly at that time they are not thinking straight at all due to certain circumstances and or situations. It would do no good to blame everyone I meet because it's not everyone's fault. Would I be angry at my parents? Yes, I would because of my situation at the time. Everyone else? Probably, even though it wouldn't prompt them to send me home. I often wondered and now I realize that the children I worked with appreciated the impact that I made on their life to some point. If only for a moment. Some of the children were so angry until it was really hard to reach them. In working with children that were not in care I found that the difference was not that great. Some children still have major struggles and problems whether they are in foster care or not, for whatever reason. Some times, when I would pray for the children that I had, I would go into my own room and cry not only with them but for them. In realizing that even with adults when we go through things its really hard sometimes and to have someone come and caress us and tell us its o.k. cry if you want to, somehow it seem to make it better—wow!! How much better you feel—well, the same thing happens with children when they hurt or are having a bad moment or day.

I believe that some Children in care often times feel that they are never heard. That no one is really listening to what they have to say. Even though, Its hard for them at times to express themselves, it would seem that they can't find the words, are ashamed, or feel that its personal and they only want to talk to their own parents. Oddly enough it's hard to talk to their own parents at times as well. I wanted to try to think how foster children might think and feel. How they may feel prompted me to do this book. They have areas that often time's foster parents can't reach, caseworkers can't reach, and even the therapist sometimes just can't seem to reach whatever it is that the child is in need of at that time. Have you ever really thought how they may feel I mean really thought about it? I think that if you could get the child to really really open up to you, you would find that there was more going on than what you thought. Do you believe that children talk to God? Well, some of them do. If you could reach into the back of the child's mind and I know we can't but if we could and he talked to God I believe it would sound something like this:

God I have to talk to you—you are the only help I have and I want you to know just how I really feel at this moment and what I am going through. God, I wouldn't be here if it were not for you. You made it possible for me to exist. I've been through so much and much to my surprise it's shocking to me that I had to go through these things. I've suffered much, things that I thought to be unfair, for a kid. I have been separated from people I love. I am not an adult so why do I have to be treated like one. I am suppose to go through kid things, someone else is suppose to deal with things that hurt me, things that make me feel sad. So, why do I have to deal with it? I don't really know how to deal with it? God help me to do the things that I need to do to survive. Amen

A beautiful and honest prayer and filled with things and circumstances that would cause tears to linger. Tears that just don't seem to want to go away. The child, when talking about his situation, as he try to explain what happened from his point of view, can you just imagine, sometimes its hard to hold back the tears. He's confused about the situation—he would like to help straighten it out but don't have the power to do so. As tears linger from one day to the next, in some children's mind I believe that this is one situation to ponder on. Just say for instance that this child was telling you his situation:

Our family was pretty close knit I thought. But sometimes you can be right in the middle of something and still not know what's going on. This is the way it was with us. We were at home right there and still didn't notice that there were problems, and that these problems were going to cause us to be removed from where we lived. If we were older we probably would have seen it coming but we didn't notice. Then all of a sudden the next thing we knew there was a knock at the door and everything it seemed turned upside down . . . I found myself screaming at the top of my voice.

"No—No—I don't want to go, let me go I want my mommy—I want my daddy, why are you doing this to me? Let me go—let me go—I hate you-I hate you, you make me sick. Kicking and screaming—fighting to stay home. What are you doing? I want my brother, I want my sister. Help!

Everything went so fast it seems. One minute I am home and the next minute I am gone. Being taken away. I am being taken away from my house and taken some place that's very unfamiliar to me. I am with people that I don't know doing and discussing things that I don't quite understand. Doesn't matter how I cry and tell them I don't want to go, they just ignore me and continue taking me to the car. My parents are arguing with them but it's not working. They are cursing—doesn't matter it doesn't stop them from taking me—from taking us. They are being asked questions and don't have any answers. They don't want to give answers. So, now I have to leave because they say things are not up to par at my house. There are many children going through the exact same thing, or something similar, or children that were beaten up, abused, neglected or were doing just fine. So many of us taken away for so many reasons none of which make sense to us. Some of us really didn't care what the situation was at home, we would just rather be home than with a group of people that we don't know. We wondered—Why do we have to be placed here? Why do we have to be placed anywhere? Then, I understood that some children really needed to be removed for their safety, well fine move them, because I don't feel like I am in danger. I really don't. Some one has made a mistake—a big one.

Why can't we just enjoy childhood? It's not suppose to be stressful for us, we shouldn't have to worry about what's going to happen to us next, what we're going to eat next, will we have a good night sleep or not, will we have changing clothes to put on, clean clothes? If we get sick what will happen to us, when danger comes who will protect us? We didn't ask to come here. We didn't ask to be born but it seems like we did because so many things happen to us its like we brought it on ourselves and no one is to blame. Our parents saw fit to do this, they brought us here. Whether they deserted us or just had a streak of bad luck, or just fair didn't do what they were suppose to, the fact still remains the same we are here and we don't like the situation that we are in, its not fair. We don't like it because some of us have suffered things that no child should have to suffer. What kind of a person would do a child the way some of us have been done? Especially, when children didn't ask to come here. It would be different if we said "Hey here we are we want to be born to you, come on make it possible—please. But we didn't. Some of us when we were taken away, our parents should have immediately done what was necessary to get us back—but they didn't—why? What did we do? Tell us, because some parents came to get their kids and some didn't—why? Some parents that I have seen never came and got their children. For the ones that do come they do this because they care and want to try to make it right. There are others that don't care at all I guess and this is why some parents don't need their children. That's because when we talk about it people say that some parents did terrible things to their children. We have always heard that there are consequences for things especially bad things. And there need to be. Not only for children for adults as well. For the parents that really want to try, it's not an easy job sometimes, but they still do it, for some of the children, parents leave them here, why? No answer. For some of us much time has passed and we're still here. If a person is not prepared to be a parent then leave children where they are. Unborn. We shouldn't have to worry about how to survive. These are things that parents are supposed to worry about not us. Some parents want to do good but the system make it so hard for them until they just give up because they feel there is no hope. Then, they sign away their rights and I can't say it doesn't hurt them because I believe for some it really does. One day everything is going along good—we're happy even though conditions may not be what someone else think they should be. People are different. People think different, people act different, people come from different places, people have different genes, different backgrounds. So why can't people be different to society? Here I am a child, no, conditions are not the best, but I am with the ones I love. Why don't they love me back? I hear adults say all the time that love is an action word. Then why can't you, my parents show me love? Why can't you do the things that make me happy? At one time I was a happy kid and to me I was doing well. One day something happened; my whole world was taken away by people I don't even know. Now I don't know what to do to fix it and if I did know could I? I don't know how to fix it; I would if I only knew how. I cry and cry in my room—and still I don't understand nor know how to fix this. I don't even know who to really place the blame on. I'm too young and everybody look over me when it's decision time. Everybody put the blame on someone else. I just sit and look and listen not necessarily agreeing but listening. Do you think I'm stupid or something, I have views and ideas about what's going on but does it matter? No. Yes, I have thoughts about what happens in my life, but they don't matter either. Am I supposed to be an invisible person with a hearing problem? I can hear you. Do you think I can't? Right now it seems I don't have a friend in this world that really care about what has happened to me. Someone please step up and take me from here so that I won't have to stay? Someone please? Again, I realize that some children have been badly abused and needed to be taken away, and even then they wanted to remain home with their families doesn't matter what they did nor what happened. These children had to be removed, too much danger. All of us were not in danger; we may not have been taken care of correctly. Other types of things could have happened that wasn't dangerous. Were parents given the opportunity to go to someone and try to get help? I don't know if they did or not, all I know is that children don't deserve this. We are supposed to be special, so special until no one should want to hurt us. All over the world children are being hurt, why? If you as an individual wanted to hurt us why did you even give birth to us? No everyone doesn't hurt children. We are so proud that there are people like that. We don't deserve the hand we are sometimes dealt.

You see we don't want to be separated we want to play with our sisters and brothers this is what we are use to doing. How are you going to just break this up? One thing that children will almost always have is each other as sisters and brothers. Can't you understand that? We are a family even without our parents if we don't have anything else we have each other.

This is why I have to pray to God in my child voice because I don't really know how to pray and ask him to help me. I have to believe that he know what I want to say, what I am trying to say, what I need to say to make it better. This all happened not because of me, because of someone else. If I could speak for all children which I can't then I would think : I am in a place where I don't belong and how do I know that this is where I need to be. Sometimes a child is made to do things that he doesn't want to do and because he is a child he can't be the deciding factor as to whether it happen or not. Why can't I say what I want? You say that you want, what's best for me—how can you know what's best for me if you don't even know what's best for you? A person make a mistake and you act like you never made one—you want to condemn them for the rest of their life, well what about your life. Had most people been condemned for things that they've done, then a person may have more compassion for someone that made a mistake once in their life and try to help them rather than put them to death so to speak. I at least understand that things happen in peoples lives that cause them to do stupid things and make mistakes—big mistakes, sometimes I got yelled at and sometimes for things that I did or didn't do, but, I don't hate anyone for it. If I could be with my parents I would tell them, "you are all I have and all I ever want why can't you just love me back? It's not asking too much. No one can ever take your place. I don't want to leave you I want to be with you please don't give me up, be patient with me, be patient with yourself, fight for me, don't let them take me, give yourself a chance to get it right. I just want things to be better. I know you have made mistakes so have lots of people. You can take care of me until I finish school and then I will leave and you will be free, if that's what you want. You have problems—so do lots of people. Society may give up on you but I won't. Never. How can you be a good example doing wrong things? This is the way some of us think and feel in our hearts. There are so many of us—and we are so hurt because things are going on around us and we don't know how to fix them. I am going to have to suffer because I don't know what to do I am too young to know what to do. If perhaps you think I am not eating then look into it and be sure that I am not eating. If by chance we need groceries couldn't you help us out just this one time maybe? Can't you just help us to get groceries? You are our neighbors, will it kill you to just give me a sandwich and not call all over the world and tell everybody? I was told that back in the day children were not taken and if they were it wasn't anything that happened on a regular basis. The neighborhoods pitched in and helped each other. Even with the kids—that's love. Whatever happen to that? And if you have to tell someone can it just be someone that will help with food, or a job? Ooops!!!!! I forgot—that would be hard to do since so many people can't just do that without it benefiting them in some kind of way. And if you did that you wouldn't be hurting my parents you would be helping them, and you certainly don't want to do that. Can you just think that a person is having a tough time right now and need a little help? Oooops!!!!!!!Again Not possible. Yes, sometimes people spend their time telling on others and they should really tell it on themselves. Be sure of what you are telling—one mistake can cause so much unnecessary pain. It's too important to play guessing games with. Please be sure of what you are saying or are accusing a person of. When it comes to the system I have to ask the question "Have you really done everything you can to reunify a family before you start removing children?" And worse than that putting them up for adoption. Even after you move them do you try? Do you want glory for destroying families? That's nothing to be proud of. If anyone would like a pat on the back for that then you can have it. Some children are taken away and then adopted, separated from brothers and sisters no visitation rights—can you feel it—can you see it happening to you? Would you like it? Oh, sure you just get over it—you can do it—you can see them when they are grown—like maybe when they are 18. Now just think who can be normal going through all this stuff?

Oh God, sometimes I look around and I see so many unhappy children. Their lives have been destroyed. Their faces are so sad and they try to hide it so no one will know that right at that moment their world is completely torn apart. They want to cry forever—that's how miserable it is. Their life is torn up, and they are not the one that did it. So many of us in different places and none of us where we really belong. You can't just fit in to something like that. How can anyone think you are supposed to just fit in like nothing has happened? How would you like to do it? Could you? Probably not. Well think about it, how you can expect me to. Nights are lonely; sometimes I can't go to sleep. It seems when I close my eyes I see family, I see the people I wish to see yet I can't. My little puppy—where is he—how is he? I don't know. I miss my family can't you see that? What part don't you understand? I open my eyes because it saddens me. I don't want to cry then someone will ask me what's wrong and I don't want to tell them because then they will began to give me all the different reasons why this happens why that happens and I don't believe a word of it. It's so hard to hold back the tears, my eyes fill and I try not to blink because I don't want sympathy—I want help. The tears fall anyway. My God my tears are lingering—they just won't go away. I want them to—why can't I believe anyone? Most of the time what we hear are lies. Promises that won't be kept. I have to try to dry my eyes and figure this out.

Let's see, o.k. here we are and you want me to just fall in here and go to sleep like nothing has happened. You bought me to a place, a house and you want me to go to sleep in this house with people I have never seen before and I am suppose to just sleep like I know they won't hurt me as well. They are afraid because they don't know what I am going to do to them if anything, and I am afraid because I don't know what they are going to do to me. I am supposed to just take that and act like everything is o.k. I don't think so—I want to be left alone and no one can understand why. Why? Can't you understand? Do you want me to answer that for you—it's because its not you—you say you understand but you really don't—you couldn't because its not you, so stop saying that you do. I am so tired of people lying to me, lie after lie—why can't you just be honest like you want me to be? So many questions—no answers. And then you wonder where kids get some of their habits, most children do what they see adults do. This explains a lot of issues that children deal with . . .

It's really a good thing that even when we think we are alone, to be reminded that there is someone some place that understand, and that person won't play like he understand and really never try to understand. Yes, it's God, and he is going to make everything alright for us. Right now it seems he is the only real, honest friend that we have. We don't really know who else to talk to or to believe. We often resent the foster parents sometimes because even though they didn't take us we believe they are just as guilty. And yes, it's the wrong way to think, but when you are angry, at times it doesn't matter how you think. This is how we feel, to the foster parent it's just a way to make money, and they don't really care about us. Sometimes, we are so angry until when we do wrong things we can't even say that we are sorry, we don't want to say we are sorry. Mainly because we think it's just for the money. Plus we don't want to make the person feel better; we want them to feel as miserable as we do so we won't apologize. We just sometimes want everyone to suffer just as we have. We want others to know what it feel like to feel as though you don't have anyone. When you feel this way you feel you are really lost. Anyone can't just fill in and make it better. It's not a job site—a game. Its life—my life, our life. And anyone can't just fill in the spaces and make it alright. That's not the way it work, because, sometimes in our life we are physically hurt. We are mentally hurt and almost destroyed. Why, because of someone else's anxieties, and frustrations. Why take your frustrations out on us. We didn't cause the problem but we have to pay for them like we did. So many things have happened to some of us, we don't understand why, and we're confused. You think you can make it go away by letting me talk to someone, therapist after therapist. Someone that look at the situation as being a job. Someone who look at the situation as a chore. Of course everyone is not like that but trust me some are. In order to help, you have to be able to put yourself in my position, that person's position. Otherwise, how can you say you can feel my pain? And stop telling me the same thing over and over—"It's not that bad, it's going to get better. You have to try and we are going to do everything we can to try to help you get back to your parents, just hang in there a while." You as a therapist or caseworker, friend, foster parent doesn't matter who but you have to literally close your eyes and imagine going down the same lane that that person went down. No you can't physically feel it but in your mind if you can clear it of some of the other things you have there—for a minute you may be able to. Then and only then can you help me. Therapist sometimes takes other peoples word about foster children and they haven't really analyzed the situation to see or try to figure out if whatever is said is the case or not. I have seen therapist order sleep medication because the foster child said he needed it and the parent said he didn't. They didn't pay any attention to the foster parent. I also saw the therapist stop a medication because the child lied and said that he didn't need it, and the foster parent didn't want it stopped because he did need it. It's all mixed up. Everyone think they know and they really don't, and what it all boils down to is that I want my mom and dad. Both of them or one of them. I would rather have them both. Why can't I have them? How can you see everything but that? If I can't have both of them then I want someone that's related to me. I know you have reasons why I can't be with them either; you say that you have good reasons why I can't. Some of the reasons good some bad. We don't know because you don't tell us anything. And this may sound wrong but it's the way I feel and the way that I am thinking. There are parents, I have seen them you told them things to do and the children could go home and they did it and the system still kept the children. Why do you do that? Oh, they finally went home, some of them, but why were you holding them? Wow, must be the money. You can say so many things and sometimes you don't do them. So why? Do you even sit down and really be concerned about my true feelings? No, let me answer that for you. Its so tiring listening to everyone, say they want to help and don't. If we go back to why we were taken away, look at this, some of us were taken away for stupid reasons. Oh shucks we had roaches, I am sure it would cost too much to have our house sprayed, of course it would of cost thousands of dollars. O my God you came to our house on a call because of nosey school teachers, yes, sometimes teachers are just out of order, dipping and dabbing where they really shouldn't, it may help sometimes but come on what does it hurt to comb a kid's hair. House dirty—good God from glory—go into some of your houses. Is yours spick and span. Parenting classes, education, cleanliness classes, why can't the government and every body concerned spend money to help reunify families instead of tearing them apart? Who are you to take us and separate us and not let us see one another until we are grown? Who do you think you are? Do you feel proud? You take so many kids you can't even keep caseworkers to work with them. You snatched us up with no clothing—nothing, some of us had nothing and then you put us in a home and expect them to go out and buy clothes, you took us why can't you go out and get clothes first? It doesn't matter to you that we are ashamed because you make us look thrown away and raggedy all at the same time. Yes, we are ashamed because we don't have anything, only the clothes on our backs. And you don't think it's embarrassing when you take some of us to someone and we go into their house with nothing. Its bad enough we are ashamed because we have to be there anyway. If you were smart you would have a clothing room with new clothes in it for us when you take us that way, or used clothes even. To us we look bad enough and you add insult to injury by taking us with nothing and if we go to bed, when we wake up in the morning we have nothing to put on. Oh, the foster parent can go and get clothes and you will give the money back. Why? You know you have a placement take money with you for that child or go to the clothing building or room and get the child clothing. Most of these comments came from children that didn't mind sharing information other children are so angry until they wouldn't even talk and they don't care, they are angry and will remain angry and foster parents can't change it and neither can you. My foster parent went through so many changes until it's pitiful. At times you have to wonder: man I am glad I am the child and not the foster parent. Just think we sit in the system day in and day out and watch and listen to everything. We don't agree at least those of us that are old enough to understand and discuss we don't always agree. Sometimes, that's what we do—talk among ourselves about different things. All children don't do that, some are afraid they will be moved.

Our lives are miserable and then, sometimes we are stuck in foster homes with foster parents whose lives are just about as miserable as ours because they want to help and you, the system seem to make it as hard as possible for them to. I think they would do much better if they were better understood and maybe paid a little more decent. We think and we wonder about things to. We sit and listen to foster parents complain and they don't seem to be happy either, caseworkers keep them mad. I wonder just how much money the state pays for us. I wonder do they think that most of it is going for the kids. Could it be? I wonder. I don't know but I just wonder how money is given to agencies each month for each child? I would be willing to bet that if you go by levels, very little money goes to the foster parents and they do all the work. We have seen foster parents that really love us and care for us—and the caseworkers ride them so until they quit. And the foster parents say that it's not us it's the system they can't stand. They are not appreciated. True. They are not even appreciated by us—most of the time and we don't mind showing it. Sometimes we can be so mean and sometimes we try to be hard—sometimes we don't. Some foster parents really do the best they can and they really care. And oh boy some do the worse that they can. Believe it or not—with the way some of them are we would rather have stayed home and been neglected. YOU SEE EVERYONE HAS LEARNED THE SYSTEM EVEN US. And everyone knows exactly what to do to get by. EVERYONE!!!!!!!!!! Sometimes I sit and I think to myself—how did I get here? The foster parent wants us to open up to them and talk to them about our life, business and what has happened to us and it's not that easy. Sometimes it can be embarrassing, sometimes it hurt. It brings tears to your eyes because it's not your fault. You think and think what could I have done to prevent this? I am just a child I didn't know how nor what to do. Some of us act up because we are angry and want to make others life a living hell like ours is right now. Did you know that even in school sometimes we are treated different by students and teachers and it's not fair. Children make fun of foster kids, not all of them but a large percentage laugh at you when you are a foster child. Children don't realize that it may be us right now but could be them later—whose to say. We didn't cause the problem but we are suffering from it like we did. And even sometimes some of the teachers lie and say that they don't make difference when they really do. It's like when they know you are a foster child its o.k. to pick on you, to yell at you, to accuse you of things. One would think that we don't have anyone, at all. Therefore, because we are in foster care you can get away with doing things to us. Well, you can't it may not be our real parents but someone care about us, and you can't just do us any kind of way. It's a good feeling when you see your foster parents showing emotions about you. I am in care and I love my parents and didn't want to be mad at them but on some occasions the foster parents were. I wondered why they were mad at my parents, I didn't understand. The more I thought about it the more I figured that it's because they didn't have us with them. They seemed like they wanted us with them, and they always came up with all kinds of excuses not to get us.

We are trying to maintain and we do want the foster parents to know that its not that we don't appreciate what they do it's just that it's not fair for us to have to go through this. We do hope they understand that we don't mean to be selfish nor ungrateful but we hurt. We want our parents and you are not them. When you think about it the foster parent have their children and they do things together and they laugh and talk and when this happens it make us wonder and want to be with our mom and dad, our sisters and brothers. It hurt, I try to enjoy with them but I can't help thinking about my own family. No, the foster parent don't treat us different, most of us but it's still hard. You see if we could visit more with our relatives it would help. How can you just take me and not let me visit with my relatives. That's another thing. Even when our relatives pass away and things happen in our family—why can't we know? Don't tell them this don't tell them that. Why can't I go to funerals? Why? who is it that don't think its in my best interest? It's my family and I love them and miss them. What's wrong with you where is your compassion? You see, We feel the system disrupt lives and this is why, we feel so angry and most of us really don't care for caseworkers. Yes, there are some good caseworkers but some of them are so hard to get along with. Some of them really try and it seems those are the ones they get rid of because they take up so much time with one child. Is it fair to be in the system and be neglected? No, it isn't. Well isn't that the reason some children are removed? Sometimes I just don't understand. It seems the harder I try the more difficult it is to realize and understand that once you are in the system it seems you just can't get out. From pillar to post it don't work over here so they just do you like you do a car if it don't work you give it back and they move you some where else to start all over again.

Once you live at one place for a long time sometimes you just don't want to move no matter what. When you do its hard to readjust and it take time. Man, foster parents trip because you may talk about the family you just left, well that's natural. What's wrong with that? After you are with them a while they are not going to want you to forget them. It should be a team effort and no one should have to be jealous. One might say that if you don't talk about the former family you can adjust to the new family. Well sometimes the old family help you to adjust to the new family because you've been there so long it's almost like real family; it's sort of like when you were first taken away. Foster parents sometimes tell you they don't mind but they really do.

Sometimes I imagine what I would be doing if I were at home and what it would be like. Let's see I think if I were at home I would probably be kidding around with my sisters and brothers. We would laugh and play games, bake cookies, chase one another. We would play hide and seek, fight each other and yes that's love, tag and just have lots and lots of fun. We would dirty up the house and mess up the beds and get yelled at. Break a window by accident or something. That would be so much fun. There is nothing like dirtying up the house and getting yelled at for doing it. That's what kids do. Can't people see how much this mean to us? I want to see my family and friends. I forgot, also, to say that you have to meet a whole new group of friends. And I guess let them know what's going on with me because they always manage to ask a whole lot of questions and patiently wait on the answer. Oh, God I want to see family—I want to go home is that so wrong? Through my tears I think, I don't want to be here and I don't care how you try no one can make me want to live here. I want to live with my mom and dad or relative. Did you know that on holidays we try to fake like we are happy and some of us don't fake we just show how unhappy we are. Everybody be going on about their business and the most important thing is that they are with their family. I stare at the Christmas tree and watch the lights flash and all I can think about is my family—my Christmas tree, my turkey and dressing, fruit cakes and pies. Foster parents may say did I ever treat you as if you were not family? Well, maybe not but that's beside the point I know I am not family. I am stressed because I am not at home and foster parents are stressed because they get rode all the time. Can you sort of see how we feel, how we think? Can you half way understand? Can you make other children not be mean to us because of who we are? We try to keep it a secret but that doesn't work. What can you do different to make a difference in what we are going through? Have you even thought about it? Well, in my heart I cry for so many reasons—do you know what they are? Is somebody listening? Please can someone at least try to make changes? Try to do this different. The one thing society can do is try to make this an easier ordeal. One may say that nothing is easy about it—no it isn't, but, there are ways you can assist in helping us to try to deal with it and make it a little bit more tolerable. Maybe, I wouldn't have to be mad all the time and with an attitude. Maybe I wouldn't mind doing things that's asked of me. Maybe I can try to deal with this situation a little better than I have been. As we reach out to society for things we cannot receive at home, nor from our families can you please make a difference? Why doesn't our family members understand how we feel? Do they feel like they don't have us and there isn't room in their perfect little life for us. Don't want to deal with our issues. Well one day I will grow up and so many people will need me—I just wonder—will I do and say the same thing—Will I? We need more foster parents to help us out—give us a chance, yes, we have problems but we wouldn't be able to make it without you. If it were not for people like foster parents we would have to live in shelters all the time. Being in a home is so much better for us. If we never ever make it back home it will sadden us and there will always be a void in our heart that no one can fill. Until some of these things can be fixed we are where we are and we will try to maintain. Our tears have a reason to linger and they do. They take breaks but they just don't go away—they linger.

Yes, we know there are foster parents that are just not cut out for the job of foster parenting. Therefore, we thank the ones that are. Also, we just want to say that we appreciate the help that we received in doing this letter it meant a lot and it mean a lot knowing that someone is going to finally hear about the things that we feel. It's easier to do when someone is not sitting there looking directly at you. We prepared a little poem to go with our portion of this book and we hope you like it. Thanks!

Can't society see—Its you that make the real difference!!!!!!!!!!!

I SIT IN A DAZE

I sit in a daze, my heart filled with fear
Wishing that someone in my family was here

With them is where I long to be
Why is that so hard for others to see?

I cry in my heart, through my eyes I can't see
There are tears there, why can't hurts just let us be?

We don't ask for much, we just want to live
We want to receive love, and have so much to give

Can you want what's best for us, and do all you can
Through whatever crisis, just help us to stand

Can you pray for us, that whatever happens to us is best?
Through Gods grace and mercy he will do the rest

A FOSTER CHILD

My Point Of View

This book was necessary to write due to my experience with the foster care system. It's somewhat emotional for me because I have seen the pain that children in care experience from past and present situations. My many years of experience as a foster parent led me to really want to make a difference or help make a difference as far as foster children and foster parents are concerned. I made a decision to stop being a foster parent for a while because I could no longer deny what I know now about the operation of the foster care system. I seriously pray that what I've experienced will help or enlighten others of the seriousness of making some type of change for the children as well as foster parents. I hope this book will enlighten others and somehow bring justice to the well being of children in care in whatever area it is needed in the system.

Because I believe that God has called different individuals and couples to be foster parents for the love and care of the children, it also lead me to believe that foster parenting is just not for everyone. It would also appear that the systems method of operation has not proven to be as beneficial or effective to the care of children possibly as they would have hoped. It seems that when an individual is asked whether or not they would like to be foster parents, some raise an eyebrow, because of misconceptions and so many other things. This is one of the reasons that it was and is very important that I try to do something to help make the change that will benefit children in care as well as foster parents. I truly pray that even this little bit of information will help and make some kind of change or impact for the children and the foster parents. I know that God put us in a place to help and when I say us I mean foster parents, and anyone else that would like to really help children and make a difference. There is a very bad need for foster parents and the need would be met, if the rules and some guidelines were different, and of course the pay scale changed. The need will never be met until there is a dramatic change in the system and in potential foster parents. The system because it make all the rules—and decide the reimbursement—the foster parent because they do all the work once the child is placed in their home basically, and its important that they decide whether or not to really be a foster parent—not guessing but know this is what they want. Its more than just a walk in the park, it's a very difficult job and in order to do it successfully you really have to think about it before you make the final decision to do it. The rules are not always agreeable with foster parents. Even though the rules are the rules foster parents need to feel that they don't have to be intimidated by opinions when it comes down to following the rules. Foster parents have to realize that we have freedom of speech and that we can speak up when we need to. You shouldn't have to be afraid that your license will be threatened if you state your case. We are not slaves to the system, where we have to only take care of the children and be quiet. A lot of the stress that some foster parents encounter comes from the fact that they feel they cannot say what they think or feel. They can't complain. A caseworker can stand flatfooted and say anything to you, talk to you like you are a child and you are suppose to just listen and not speak. Not true. Whenever you have something to say—say it. The caseworker's job is not to look down on you because of that question or statement but to correct you if you are wrong and explain or discuss whatever is going on. They only have a job and all of them are not happy with it or the rules. A foster parent should never just sit and not say anything especially if they have concerns or if they did not agree with something that was done or said—you should be allowed to discuss it. You really may not agree with everything the system do just like they don't agree with everything we as foster parents do, and don't mind telling us. Some of our tactics differ from theirs but that does not mean that ours are wrong and theirs are right just because of who they are. Nor does it mean that ours are right and theirs are wrong. That's one of the problems that happen it seems pretty often in the world as a whole, and that is that there are too many chiefs and not enough Indians. If everyone gives orders there will be no one to take them. When looking at caseworkers and when they come to your house for whatever the reason, I don't believe that upon arrival they should be disrespectful to the fostering parents under no circumstances. It is the caseworker's job to go into an individual's house and respect that person and their house. No foster parent should have to experience anyone coming to their house and talking to them any kind of way just because they are a caseworker, supervisor or any other kind of worker. It could even be a regular adult it really doesn't matter. Respect is something you give especially if you want to receive it. Foster parents should be respectful as well, and most of the time they are because of that fear I spoke about earlier. If something has been done wrong, something so bad until you can't discuss it and your accusations are correct then you come, tell an individual what's going on and if you are going to remove children then do that. No one have the right to talk to an adult like a child especially in front of a child—think about it, you wouldn't want them to talk to you that way. Children often times and most times watch adults—their ways and actions and take it from there. They are the first ones to throw it in your face when you try to tell them not to do something; they are quick to remind you that you did it. It's therefore, important that foster parents are talked to as adults. It's only fair that others are treated the exact same way when confronted by foster parents, with respect. When a foster parent lashes out at a caseworker for treating them otherwise they are well within their rights. You give what you want—respect.

In the beginning of the book I tried to take you through a journey into the heart of a foster child. When I say in the heart I simply mean I tried to feel what it appear that child might feel, think as he might think and be able to better help the child as well as try to understand him or her better. Have you really ever thought about the role of a foster parent? The role of a foster child? Have you ever tried to feel what the children feel or did you just never even think about it? Even if you try to put yourself in the place of the caseworker, I am sure that a lot of the things that they do they are not satisfied with doing them. I would suspect that they don't care for all the rules either—but it pay the bills. That I feel I know because of conversations I have had with several. If you never gave it a thought maybe you will now. It's so important, now unless you lie on someone big, some organization big, or do something really deadly bad its hard to get the right media outlet so that you can be heard and someone will take notice. Hopefully this way we can all be heard—children, foster parents, grandparents, wage earners and caseworkers as well

We as a people could try to reach out and check out the situation and see what's really going on with foster children. With foster parents. Show an interest, send in concerns and comments. When asked shouldn't everyone be treated equally fair? You look at the fact that fair is a pretty big word for some. Fair doesn't always work because it's the last thing that some people want to do and that is treating an individual fair. When I think of the whole situation as a foster parent and even now that I am no longer a foster parent, a lot of it just doesn't make sense. When you think about it and you began to put certain things together, logically speaking it just doesn't make sense any way you might look at it. No one it seems is being treated as they should be. Someone is always being enslaved to the system one way or another. You see it's hard to satisfy some people and it doesn't matter what you do. People being those surrounding the foster care system. Being enslaved—basically would mean much work—no comments—no complaints—keep them to yourself if you have any, just do your job and if there is something you don't like you except it and deal with it and most of all leave it alone.

These are my views and in talking with other foster parents I found that they feel almost the exact same way. Some are fostering children with attitudes, attitudes because even though they want to help, the compensation is not nearly enough for the work, so they try to maintain and do the work anyway. Ask yourself—Would you? Compensation is always going to be an issue not only with foster care, but in all walks of life. People want more money for their work. That's what you do, you work you get paid. You can't blame foster parents for wanting more either. I have heard so many people say oh heck no—no amount of money could make me do that. What's that? Raise someone else's child? Be bothered with someone else's child. I don't think so, its too much work and the system don't pay you nearly enough they don't even come close. No one else's child is going to live in my house and curse me out, or tear up my things, and make me like it. Now believe it or not this is a typical response when you ask some people about foster care. They see what some foster parents go through and they also see the benefits, unfortunately what they see foster parents go through out weigh the benefits. So they choose not to do it.

Foster parents are here for the children. When we get children we try our very best to feel what the child feel. No, we can't fully but we have some idea. When a child is taken away it doesn't matter what the reason is. There's so much hurt. Why? So much pain. Why? So many tears. Why? Because their heart has been ripped out. As with hurt, pain, and other emotions they do not discriminate. They take up space in anyone's heart, and just sit there or take root and grow causing all kinds of problems. So, they also do the same thing to children. Our job—we have to help make it better. We have to try to move these hurts and pains. So, the decision has been made you decided to do this—to take on this job so that's what you do—you get to work and do what ever you can to try to make life better for the children.

A foster parent has to learn certain things about each child that they work with. It really doesn't matter if its foster care or day care, you do what you have to do to be able to fulfill the need of the child. If there is something special that has to be done to the hair, you learn and you do it so the child looks nice. If you don't know what to do then you ask someone you don't just let the child's hair look any kind of way just because you don't know what to do with it. You find out the foods the child like or dislike—have had or have never had—you learn and you don't mind. Yes, some things you may not know how to make so you ask other foster parents or use a cookbook. This is what you do, not to prove a point but because you really want to do what you can to make the child feel special, loved and at home, even though he may not see this as his home with his family you want to make him feel as close to home as you can, or that he will allow. You don't want him to feel different. A handout on hair care with different ethnic children would be helpful. A food list may even be helpful. Of course one might say; I'm not going through all that, he can eat what I fix or don't eat at all. First, that's the wrong attitude. Well, put yourself in that child's place, he might eat what you prepare, but if we bought what the child like at the store, already prepared if you don't know how to prepare it, you are only trying to do something that the child would enjoy. You don't have to do it all the time just sometimes maybe so the child will think or even feel that you care about his feelings. There are times when the children have a difficult time being comfortable with a foster family that's not of the same nationality as they are, so you have to put forth a special effort to try to make them feel welcome. It can make a really big difference as far as how things turn out. When you make that special effort to try to make things work it will in turn make the child feel special and cared for more. If by chance it doesn't work, at least you really tried.

There are times when children that have been at your home for a while—upon the arrival of newcomers will try to make the new children think that you make difference in children. You have to have a remedy to stop it before it has the chance to get started. When one has been there longer than the other, sometimes that child tend to think that he should get special treatment or special attention, maybe even special privileges, and have a fit if you don't give them to him or her. It helps to make that child aware that we don't love nor care for one child any more than the other and that it was a waste of time to try to put you to the test to see if you do indeed make a difference. That way no one would believe that they had special privileges. As the day or night progress you wouldn't have to deal with this problem because they tend to throw it in each others face who has the most privileges and why. Children are smart and sometimes try to get away with whatever they can, and most of the time its privileges because of whom they are and how long they have been there. Again, children watch everything and pay close attention to everything, listening to all that they can. They will also watch facial expressions and try to read them. However, if you think on the best way to go about doing things involving children in care you always have to be so careful because the smallest of things can get you written up, due to the fact that it would seem you get written up for everything anyway. Because of this fact some foster parents are on pins and needles constantly. When children hear all the things that are against us coming from a caseworker, that in turn give the child more to work with. It sometimes work as artillery or ammunition for the child against the foster parent. The foster parent then have to be watchful with guards up at all times even when they don't have to be. One might say—why? If you are not doing anything wrong then you don't have to worry about it. Yes, you do. Think about it—when you are dealing with an individual that's always looking for something to complain about and you don't want to have to deal with that person, you try to stay on your toes only to find that they dig up something anyway. The slightest mistake can cause you to be written up or loose your license.

If you really think about it, we could use citations, and in being a foster parent it would appear that most foster parents could probably write their own book on a subject like citation whys and how comes. The reason being because you get written up for just about everything. I was once cited for something that wasn't my fault and asked to sign the form that the organization used and I told them I would not sign it because I didn't do anything wrong and to sign it would be saying that I was guilty. It's so easy to write someone up or charge them with doing something especially when you are not that person being charged. You have to understand that yes, foster parents sometimes have hard times with some of their children because of what they were and are going through. Therefore, its not unusual for foster parents to make mistakes. When I tried to put myself in the child's place it was to try to imagine how I would feel if it were me. I would feel and probably act like the child was acting. I might have acted worse. You can't just expect a child to act much better than what they are acting considering what that child has gone through. It can't be that easy. Can you imagine? Probably not.

If taken into consideration how much work the foster parent has to do, one could better understand the task that stands before that parent. It seems even when you feel you are doing your very best its just not good enough. It can become a discouragement even a resentment. You began to resent the fact that you became a foster parent. So many foster parents would get out but foster parents sometimes get caught up in several ways and find it hard to get out and just quit. Some foster parents bite off more than they can chew—some have bonded with the children, the children have bonded with them and they want to try to keep them in spite of that because they love them, some want to prove a point—that I can change this child, when no one else could, and want the world to know, or just for the money. Whatever the reason it's a job doing it, the number of children is rapidly growing, therefore, we need a lot more people to help to make a difference in these children's lives.

When we say that it is a job being a foster parent, we don't say it to complain because this is something you choose to do you are not forced to do it. Without the foster parent where would the children go? Shelters run out like prisons do—all the time. Without foster parents they will have to build more shelters which they will probably have to do anyway. Foster parents go through many things while fostering children and at times it would appear that no one really cares. One would ask "Why do they do it? Because someone has to do it. Believe it or not some foster parents want to make a difference in some child's life. And yes, some people do it for the money and the money only, and really couldn't care less about the children. I am not saying that there are not bad foster parents—of course there are bad ones but I believe that the good ones out weigh the bad ones. We as a people have to do as we would do with anything else when a strategy has to be decided to change anything else for the better. There just have to be better ways of screening, more in dept interviews, more references. We have to try harder to come up with a plan to try to straighten out this situation. I believe we will always have more children than we have foster parents to care for them. There are children that have been in the system forever and these children rely on foster parents and the system for their well being.

Because all foster parents are not good ones and because the system does not always do as they are suppose to either some children probably would of learned more if they would of stayed at home. Even with this concept you have agencies that will tell you well we have to wonder if you are doing foster care for the money—and one foster parent said, "Well of course you are doing it for the money, you would have to be crazy to do it for free." If there has to be a difference then that difference would be that some foster parents really care about the children that they keep. Because it entails so much work, so much running from here to there, yes, it's worth something and some foster parents really do their job. When I say that, I can't stress enough that it's worth something to do what a foster parent do. No one can pay a foster parent what it's really worth for what they do. But we as a people that is supposedly so concerned could try. You have to keep in mind that with this type of work will also come different types of stresses. You have bad days just as anyone else does. All of your days are not good all the time. And this is typical of almost anything. Sometimes when you look at what's expected of foster parents you would think they are the real parents. The real parents have it made in the shade it would seem. Sometimes, I think the system deal with cases of mistaken identity. The case workers forget that we are the foster parents not the real parents. Therefore, the things they expect of us and say to us need to be done to the real parents and the children may not have been removed in the first place.

This is why it's worth something. It's not the foster parent's intentions to ever turn our back on our children. Sometimes, we are put into situations where it would appear that this is what's going on and no one is going to straighten it out for us. Let the child go ahead and believe that we turned our backs its o.k. If you look at it from a good foster parent's point of view you figure:

When a child's world is turned upside down because someone ran in and tore it up, we step in and try to help put it back together again. We are the ones that go back and forth to the schools and monitor the children, we step in when there's a problem at school or anywhere with the children and we don't treat them like they are foster children. We stay up with them at night when they're sick, like we did our own—those of us who have children. We take them to the doctor when they are sick and sit there no matter how long it take until they are done. If they have to go in the hospital we sit and spend nights with no problem. When there's something going on in the neighborhood where people are upset we take up for our children and we don't uphold them in the wrong, we do whatever is necessary to make it right. You see a good foster parent would not allow anyone to come in their yard and jump all over their children for doing anything; you should go through the foster parent first. That is the way I handled mine and if I said it was o.k. for you to talk to my child then you could, otherwise you would have to go home, or talk to me. We have to make sure that our children are safe. Foster parents put their neck on the line all the time. The children have to know that we have their best interest at heart. Yes, as long as we are caring for them that make them ours. We have to make sure our kids are safe, and that they feel safe. Depending on what the child came out of that sometimes isn't an easy chore. When they get into trouble and some of them do, big trouble we try to help. Some of the kids need extensive therapy due to dramatic experiences and things they have gone through. And yes, sometimes it doesn't work we may not have what that child need and if we have to give that child up speaking for myself, I try to do what's best for the child even if it mean giving him up. I don't just give up a child I try to find out where he or she is going and whose there. I am not by any means trying to pin metals on foster parents even though some of us deserve them. Yes, there are foster parents that are not what they should be just like there are parents the same way. There are more that are than that are not. I cannot repeat that enough. Just as there are caseworkers that are not what they should be, but there are also good caseworkers that really try to understand and help the foster family. I didn't get out because of the children. I got out because I didn't care for the things that are going on in the system when it comes to foster care. And yes, one day maybe I will be a foster parent again but right now no. Right now I have a great need to make a difference. It's more important to me to do what I am doing and that is, try to make a difference for the children and the foster parents. You see almost everyone when dealing with foster parenting have someone that's for them—except the foster parent. Wouldn't it be nice if there were advocates for foster parents? That's one of the things we are going to be working on. The children have them even though some of them are a real pain and still need to be in training. They supposedly represent the children. Even they too sometimes use foster parents as punching bags. Someone has to make sure that foster parents don't get mistreated. We don't proclaim that we are perfect. Yes, we make mistakes, miss an appointment, miss giving a pill, give the pill later than what you should. These are mistakes that anyone can make. Well, please don't you may lose your license? I know of many mistakes caseworkers make but they still have jobs. Remarks made that were not appropriate or in the line of duty but they still have jobs. And people question why it's hard getting foster parents—think about it.

I really don't know if anyone ever thought about how the system hurt the children and foster parents. Look at the fact that therapy will work best on an individual that want help, and this is my belief. When children are angry and don't care they couldn't care less about therapy. They just sit and look at the therapist like he or she is the one that need help. Pills, pills, pills, potential drug addicts. I will never ever believe that every child that come into foster need to be on pills. So many drugs. Some children be so high they don't know if they are going or coming, sitting in a daze, sleep in class, not responsive at home. How the heck is he suppose to learn anything when he can't half see the board and his understanding is altered because of drugs. Oh, of course there are children that make good grades while on meds, graduate from school, go on to college but there are also those that don't—lots of them. Yes, as with the regular drug addict the high temporarily take away the capacity to think on what ever it is bothering the person, it also satisfy the craving the body have for the drug. Whatever it is bothering an individual is gone for a while or it's not as bad as it was but once the high wears off they are right back where they started, with the same problems and maybe more. When the child is able to one day get out of foster care, sometimes children go and look for drugs that have the same or similar effect because this is what the child is use to. It can cause the child to do criminal things and his life is then ruined for sure. He has to deal with police, jail and other types of trouble. This does not mean that all the children do the same thing; some choose not to do it. Still the system has now turned a great number of children into drug addicts. Some of their actions will not be desirable ones. Whether in the system or not it can be a terrible thing. We as adults have to realize that children in care have to try to deal with the fact that their world has been torn to pieces. It's a struggle but, with help sometimes they can better deal with it without drugs. Its like adults being sick everything does not call for drugs just some things. So, all children don't need medication just some of them and when the child is able to maneuver without the meds take them off. You have to keep in mind that children are like adults in many ways even though they are children. For instance, they have the right to be left alone if they so choose sometimes. Sometimes, when they are in a daze they are just thinking like adults do. It doesn't mean that they are contemplating suicide, or that they are gone haywire. They have to deal with separation, they have to deal with loss, and they have to deal with other things that they are going through. The fact that they are separated from siblings, and they don't want to be is a huge problem. The more one think on this situation the more terrible it seems and the more a person should want to help children. Just think about children that have been told they will never see their siblings again. Probably until after they are 18 or so. Can you imagine? This is a major problem, and a terrible thing to tell a child. It happen to children all the time and you have to ask—how can anyone do that? Who make that decision? The courts? Who? Well, obviously whoever make the decision to make that happen don't care either. It's a hurt that most children cannot get over. Why would anyone want to do that? I would guess that keeping the kids where they can see each other would cost the system too much money. It would mean paying for foster care services for as long as necessary. Don't you think a child's happiness is worth that? I often think about the system, and it spends unlimited amounts of money needlessly. Unnecessary things. Why can't more money be used for foster care purposes? It cannot be stressed enough the importance of helping and supporting these children the very best that we know how. Its o.k. to help children elsewhere but what about our children right here in our city? Our own state?

If one would meditate on the well being of our children you would have to look at and analyze what they have gone through and what they are going through. You would look at some of the things that have already touched their young life. In many good ways and some bad. When children have to just pick up and leave from where they are use to being for whatever reason it bring about a change in attitude. It's confusing to the child and often times they feel that it's not fair. It really doesn't matter how you try to explain the change, sometimes it just doesn't make sense to the child.

So, as one might see the child has already gone through a large amount of things. This means that there are certainly issues that have to be dealt with. This is why no child should be labeled as a basic child. What is a basic child? Lets see, if you go by what a foster parent see, I would think that basic means you have very few if any, issues. I would think that one is practically, in pretty good condition. No therapy. Now, even though the child has next to no issues, but do have some and he still have a mouth so he eats, he still have a need for clothes, money for school programs, special school outfits, outings to go to and etc. So in essence in order for a basic child to really be taken care of properly, he has to act up to keep his levels raised otherwise he could loose his placement. That's due to the fact that there are not many foster parents that want to care for a child that is leveled as basic. Why? Too much work, still. Lots of times some foster parents will say that the child is doing things that he is not doing so as to keep his levels up. This will keep him from being dropped to basic. When the child is basic and even moderate and otherwise the extra things that he need, the foster parent have to use their own money to supply it. Have you seen the way some foster children dress? They wear the best of clothes. Yes, some of them you have to wonder where the money is going but come on most of them dress really nice. If they don't that's when the complaining need to start to the foster parent. When foster parents tell you that if he is basic they will not keep him they are not saying this to be mean it simply mean that they know they are going to be doing lots of work for almost a little of nothing. They already know that they are going to wind up spending their own money mostly. The child is the one that gets hurt because it's not his fault. A child should not have to lose anything just because he chooses to be a better child or because he has gotten rid of some or all of his issues.

You see, it's such a joy when you have the opportunity to watch a child make real progress. You feel really really proud knowing that you played a major role in this transition. When you have a caseworker that has played a major role as well, you can feel good together. It make you feel really good. Some caseworkers are like that they will go out of their way to help you and the child. Others don't. The ones that do it seems don't last long, supposedly they take up too much time on one child. It make a big difference when the caseworker comes out and do what they are supposed to do and then some. We feel that too many times we as foster parents are expected to be perfect and without mistakes. There are so many things that would make a difference—a big difference. For instance when a child is placed in your home, why can't the money that's given for the child's clothes be given to you when they bring the child? Maybe a few days after arrival. The foster parent has to spend their money and be reimbursed in most cases. There should already be clothing some place for the children. Then, they feel like you need to keep that child first and get reimbursed the following month. If the money is reimbursement then why are you expected to use it on the children and yes, it's a big deal and it would help if foster parents could get some understanding. In many cases this is what foster parents are told. I would like to think that reimbursement means getting a refund for services rendered. If you use the reimbursement for the children which is what most foster parents are told, and that is that the reimbursement is for the children. If that be the case then where is the reimbursement for the foster parent for services rendered. Now then, I just suppose that we are keeping the children for free simply because we are desperate to do foster care and so desperate to the point that we are willing to do it for free. We just feel like doing free baby sitting. Now, if children are getting benefits for their care say for instant Social Security benefits—why can't it be used for the child's care? Fine, you guys want to save it for him well that's great and the foster parents are still under paid. If the child is a teenager he should be allowed at least a couple hundred dollars extra at least twice a year to buy extra things for himself. He's growing up give him credit for that. Child support for instance, where does it go—if the parents are paying it. I have even heard parents ask the same question. Why can't it be used for the child? If the money go back into the system as repayment for monies given to foster parents that would be great. But, by the same token if its not then it should be given to the child for clothing and other needs. Supposedly the money is so that the child can have a fairly good life as he becomes as adult. If the foster parents are under paid and you can use basic care children as an example—the money would better help take care of the child and his or her needs because the state is not compensating as it should or as it would be expected.

Apparently the state or those representing, are not taking the best of care of the child—so, therefore they need the child support now. Otherwise, how could you think kibbles and bits is enough to take care of teenagers? Most people in different agencies think they really know about the care of the child. Let me enlighten you the only one that really know is the one that's taking care of the child, the one that has spent time with the child. Even the therapist is in a place to know more than the caseworker. You can do guessing games all you like, but the only one that really know, is the one that is taking care of the child. That would be the one that's with the child more. Yes, some foster parents know children better than their real parents, and that's because even though a child is at home that doesn't mean that that parent is there with that child day in and day out. When he is taken away and began to spend time with foster parents they learn the child. Some parents work all the time and don't take time to really know their child. Books work good in some cases but not all cases.

Some of the children have been hurt so very very bad, until It's really hard to break through the wall that they have set up. Sometime, even after all you do they still have the wall—even after the therapy? It's not our fault that they still have it. It doesn't mean that we are not effective. Can you see my point? Maybe not, but none the less there is definitely a problem within the system. Yes, no one is perfect and everyone make mistakes but, the thing about mistakes that make it not so bad to make them is when you correct them and don't keep repeating them. Children don't ask to be in the position that they are in. Sometimes, when they are taken away they don't even know why, and if they are of age they have a right to know. Don't tell them this don't tell them that—well heck who are you protecting—the parent? You? Us? Who? Sometimes the very thing that hurt you can help you better than any therapist ever could. Sometimes if you knew what was really going on you could better understand it, its not as confusing. When you think of therapist, yes, the therapist do their job and yes, they help a whole lot but even with them there are limitations to how many children they can help. The same thing hold true for the foster parent. We make a difference for some but not for everyone. Some children are just not trying to give in; they are angry and intend to stay that way until they go home. There has to be a way—a better way to go about doing this. It would seem that some of the money the State give to agencies who don't give it to the foster parents—and when they do—very limited and in very small amounts—but still that small amount can go towards rehabilitating dysfunctional families. Help reunify a family. You say the house is not up to par well the money being paid for the children could repair several homes—Come on now there has to be a better way to go about this than what's going on now. It would be so wonderful if children could be reunified with their families. More and more children are coming into care and it's hard to get someone to do the parenting. Mention foster parenting and some people run and are shouting no all at the same time. This is how people think, they look at the issues the children might have. A child that can't sleep at night because of nightmares from an incident that happened while he was at home. The child has a really bad attitude at everybody except the one that caused the problem in the first place. Children that are so very different and have completely different attitudes, and mentalities. It's not the child's fault. The child feel bad as it is and we certainly don't want to add to it. So we do what we can. Sometimes our hands are tied. We can't do any more than what we've done. It's not a good feeling when you feel like you were not effective.

Children always expect adults to have all the answers and we don't always have them. Sometimes my children asked me things I wish I could answer but I couldn't. Due to the fact that most of the time the foster parents doesn't know anything. We are never informed about anything much. They would always want to know when am I going to see my mother—my dad—sister—brother. I don't know I don't have an answer for you, maybe the caseworker can tell you whenever he or she comes. Whenever could be a week after drop off—two weeks after dropoff—a month after drop off and here you are with a child with a zillion questions and you can't answer any of them. It's not fair. Children are not stupid. Foster parents are left to deal with these questions and then, when you try to answer them sensibly and sometimes with the wrong answer because you weren't told anything either, then, you are caught up in a lie because it didn't happen like you told them it would. So, you were put in a position where you told a lie and now the child has to wonder can they trust you at all since you already lied to them, and they think you are just as bad as the parent that lied or the caseworker or the therapist or anyone else that has lied to them. Sometimes my children went through things and it took all I had to try to console the child and hold the tears back in my own eyes because it hurt so bad to see what the child was going through. I kept telling God I can't do this anymore it hurt too badly. I can't stand it—how can anyone do a child this way? What is wrong with the system? What is wrong with the parents? I couldn't tell who was the most angry me or the child—smile. The children would sometimes laugh at me because I would say supposedly to myself but out loud "Man they make me so sick, I gotta get out of this, I can't stand the way they do kids." I can't stand the way they do us. There's only so much an individual can stand. When looking at children I couldn't stand to see them when they cry and look sad, it would almost kill me. Most of the time I just wreck my brain trying to figure out a way to make it better and at times I couldn't think of anything that would actually work.

You see I can't say the money didn't matter you have to have money to live I don't care who you are. You have to have money to take care of the children. I once heard an individual say that all money is not good money and that's true. Sometimes you have to go through too much for the money. You find yourself asking "Is it worth it? Sometimes the answer is no. It's all because of the discouragement that you feel. You think in your mind I am giving the children up, but I haven't made the difference in their life that I wanted to make. I changed my mind several times about having a child removed. I wanted to make sure that I did everything I could to try to help that child. We as foster parents put our feelings on hold many times. Some children in care try to spare your feelings and some don't. It's not a situation where the foster parent can afford to let feelings take top priority. You can get cursed out talked ugly to any of that and you don't be a happy camper when you do. No, I didn't like it and I wanted the child to know that I didn't like it I knew that if I stood flat footed and allowed this to happen who knows what will happen next. There has to be consequences. Oh, you didn't know they sometimes curse you out? Well they do. You still try to help them and it could happen again and again—you may be able to make a difference and maybe not. It doesn't mean that you are not a good foster parent if you can't. Point being that you as a foster parent also have feelings, the child need to know that you have feelings. The system need to know that we as foster parents have feelings. You can attend classes and workshops all day long and you are still not treated like you have feelings. Most of the time we are sitting there looking at the caseworker like am I not suppose to have feelings or something? You are sitting here complaining and constantly telling me what I am doing wrong from your point of view—well what am I doing right? Anything? Why don't you worry us to death telling us how good we are doing like you do when you tell us how bad we are doing? We care.

Some children if they hadn't been taken away who knows what would have happened. Yes, we applaud the system when they step in on time. And we frown when they don't. The key here is that everyone make mistakes no one is exempt. When you are perfect you don't take away children that should have stayed at home. Children have sometimes been taken away for no reason, really. Whatever the reason if the child is taken away it's your job to see that all of his needs are met, not some of them. Caseworkers play a big part in that. Some of the caseworkers are glad to play that part, oh to happy to do more for the children but are not allowed to. Every chance they have to do extra things, they do. That's some of them not all of them. They come out to the house and literally try to become a part of the child's life as well. I don't believe that everything should be hid from the children. Tell them the truth, I am not into faking. I try to be as honest as I possibly can with my children without hurting them. They really appreciate that. Sometimes, the child has a really bad attitude and if you have a really bad attitude I find it doesn't help when you and child have the same problem. We as foster parents have to keep our attitude in check. Let me stop right here for a moment and explain this so as to clear up a question or two. Yes, foster parents get angry; yes foster parents get angry at the kids—our own and children in care. Yes, some foster parents say things they shouldn't out loud or to themselves. Some foster parents you can't tell who curse the most them or the children. Some foster parents need therapy just like the children. It doesn't help them any more than it does the children, if they don't let it. So you see foster parents are human. And stress don't care who it rest in as mentioned before. I said that because you always have people looking for error and something to accuse foster parents of. Some of the therapist are so stressed until its sad but, they hang in there. For some therapist do you think they look tired and have bags under their eyes for nothing? Its for the ones that do. They take some of this stuff home with them just as a periodic caseworker do. It's better to me for everyone in question to just lay everything on the table with love and in love, not always with an attitude. Attitudes don't help anyone. Can you half-way see what children go through? Can you half-way see what foster parents go through? Someone has to make a difference. Someone has to make changes. Foster parents are willing to even try to continue to be foster parents in spite of all that they go through. Even when their funds are being tampered with, and this is normally enough to make anyone throw in the towel, some foster parents still hang in there. My belief is when a foster parent has done a months work he shouldn't have any problem being reimbursed. It shouldn't be late, it should be as early as possible simply because the work has been done. There should never be a "If you don't turn in your paperwork you don't get paid, what in the world do that have to do with the fact that you just completed a months work, and you deserve to be reimbursed. No one, no one has the right to hold your money I don't care what you did or didn't do because you have spent money and used utilities and groceries all month long—you have made it possible for some one else's child not to want for anything—do that not count for anything?

If by chance you have an organization that don't do a lot of the things talked about, that's good better yet that's wonderful we applaud you, that you don't do your foster parents that way. You should have no problem growing because one thing a foster parent is looking for is an agency that will support them and help them be better foster parents and not cut them up one side and down the other every time you turn around. Tell me, what good is it to give a foster parent a bonus or extra money if you have to dictate to them how to spend it? After all it is suppose to be reimbursement. Please keep in mind the meaning of the word reimbursement. Now, supposedly if when this extra money is given it is suppose to be something like a reward for service. If this is true wouldn't it seem better to just give it and let a foster parent decide how to spend it. They are entrusted supposedly to do everything else that has to do with the child why not that? Again, it would help if the rules were revised. Think about it if you are a caseworker—what impact have you made on a child's life? If you are a parent—what impact have you made in a child's life? In your child's life? A foster parent—what impact have you made? Just ask yourself this question. If you have made an impact in any child's life, that's wonderful. You see most people don't even get involved, whatever the caseworker say that's it. You just can't do that you have to have input especially when it concern a child that's in your care. When you have a child in your care you are constantly looking for ways to make it better. Ways to do it better, that's what a good foster parent does. That's what a good caseworker does.

When looking at situations if you know that something is right then you stand for that thing. You argue the point if necessary, you don't just agree to whatever someone else says to settle it. You don't agree with everything you hear.

When it comes to the child, me personally I will back the child up no matter what. If he is wrong I will do all that I can to see that it is corrected. I will fight for the child most good foster parents do. Sometimes you will find that you have to do it when dealing with caseworkers as well, the caseworker might recommend one thing and if you don't think that that is what's needed then let them know, after all you take care of this child. In speaking with other foster parents and adults there were so many things that came up in discussion, the comments and questions are numerous. Too numerous to list but here are a few:

1. Some wanted to know, how a child can be in foster care and the Parent is not made to pay child support?
2. How can women whose children are already in care be allowed To continue having children for the system to take and pay for and not be made to pay a fine, child support or nothing? Why?
3. How can children remain in care for years and the parents still have rights? How? Why do they need rights? They should of lost them when they refuse to get their kids back.
4. Why would the system separate children and put one or two of them up for adoption? Just leave the rest hanging. Why?
5. The system is hard on dead beat dads, what about dead beat Moms? They need to be hard on them to, why aren't they?
6. Why, can a caseworker threaten a child and the foster parent can't? What difference does it make as far as who make the threat it's still a threat?
7. How can you want foster parents to have all these shots and TB test before the child come and not do it with the child? Couldn't the child be infected with something as well?

8. If a foster parent have someone helping them with their children on a regular basis, shouldn't they be made to take test and have check-ups as well?

9. Who decides what the level of care reimbursement should be? Do they have children?

10. Some agencies allow foster parents to receive food stamps and other benefits—why for the ones that don't is this so wrong? You may say because they get reimbursement to care for the child, but the reimbursement is suppose to be for the foster parent isn't it? Or is it?

11. If the reimbursement is not enough which its not and if you don't want foster parents to get food stamps? Why don't you? raise the reimbursement and they won't have to?

12. Is it true that if a child has issues the therapy don't always help?

13. In reading this book information and listening to the discussions the system should be applauding the foster parents instead of riding them, don't you think?

Many more questions just like these are the ones people want answers to. They all make sense. If you think, when a child is removed from his home and need to be in a foster home wouldn't one think that that child need to be placed according to that child's need? Not just stuck where they can find space. There are several reasons that will be specified as to why the child has to be placed there. There should also be concern as far as what the child is in need of. Each child's need is different. Very few are similar. Whatever the need it's our job to make sure that it's taken care of. If the child have more extensive needs or care then it's our job to try to take care of that also. Our recommendation should be considered as to what the child is in need of; after all we are the ones that take care of that child. The caseworkers will tell us that they are taking into consideration what we are saying the child need and do just the opposite. It has happened many times. The therapist recommend something for the child and when it is brought to the attention of the caseworker, they don't follow through. They may do something entirely different. It's called neglect. So, what make you any better than the parent that neglected the child's needs?

These children need our help and that is the reason for this book, I have to try to make a difference for the children as well as the foster parents. If the therapist make a recommendation and it's in the best interest of the child, it's your job being caseworkers to follow through, especially when you know it's the right thing to do. You don't just sweep it under the rug and place that child in another foster home. It happen to foster parents all the time—foster parents have had incidents where the caseworker was told what was going on with the child and the child wanted help, the therapist said the child needed the extensive help, the child admitted that he needed help and wanted it and they immediately placed him in another foster home. It was recommended that he not be placed there. He or she would still have the same problem. Questions, questions with hardly any answers. There has to be help for us.

There has to be a better way to do this. I may not be the smartest person in the world and I may not know just what procedure to take as far as making it better, but I'm trying. I hate the way children are being done, being separated. Our society and government is so quick to help people from everywhere else—what about the people right here in this country. It's not to say that we can't or shouldn't help anyone else but our children need help as well. When we get to the point that we don't give a darn about our own family, our own city, our own state, our own country—then we have a real problem. So then it would appear that we have a serious problem. What do that tell people elsewhere about us? Our children are in need. What do we do? We have to come up with a remedy to help the children. They did not ask to be here, so why should they have to suffer for being here? The foster care system is not shrinking its getting larger with more and more children in shelters, all over the world. More and more children abused. The country spends millions of dollars locking up people for petty crimes when we have another crime to consider—child neglect, and not only from their parents from the system as well. From some of the very people that are locking up individuals for a little of nothing. Its neglect when you place a child anywhere and do not provide the necessary funds to care for that child. More family members would step up to the plate to help with children if they could get help financially with that child. You can't just expect a family member to step in and take on children or a child even with no support. Why would anyone think that that is fair? One would say that that child is your family you should be happy to care for him or her. Yes, most of them are happy to help when they are compensated. They don't stop eating and having needs because they are family. If a foster parent can be reimbursed why not a family member? If the family member was reimbursed it may be easier for them to step in and leave more room for other children that are not as fortunate at that time to have a family member that can take them. Depends on how an individual look at the situation. As far as the reimbursement for that child even with a family member, again reimbursement should not be lower than moderate. When a child is anywhere other than a foster home or with family he almost has to be moderate. So why drop it when he goes to a foster home. In another facility he's specialized, but when removed to a foster home—moderate. Think about it; do you as a people, in control of agencies and children not think that a foster parent deserve more?

I can't say and will not say that I have an answer, but I am sure the government, the state, the city have an answer. They have an answer for everything. Be it right or be it wrong. But the point still remain that there is a serious problem. And this problem has to be dealt with. Who has taken a look at the foster parent? No one. Does anyone care? Well, someone just might . . . All the system need with the foster parent mostly is for them to do the work as cheap as possible. Have you ever tried to work with a person that has other peoples genes, other individuals background—all of that. Who know what to expect. Well, caseworkers don't because all they do mostly is place the children and paperwork. They will tell you don't say this don't say that well you better say something if you intend to keep a safe environment for your child or any child. If you raise your voice you may just loose your license. Please don't let the child say you hit him or her—in front of the firing squad you go, whether you did it or not. No questions. If the system is protecting the child, why then can he be in the system all his life and become a teenager and have so many things missing that he should of learned as a child and didn't. He was in the states care as a child, what happened. Who is monitoring the children making sure that they are getting everything they should be getting in school? Who can afford to make these kind of mistakes? He is almost grown now and so many things are missing. He won't even know what to do when the system throws him out. And the system will let him go and he will be on his own and not knowing anything. He won't have a clue as to what he is supposed to be doing. Who is doing the neglecting now? Who will you answer to? Can't you see it; the system is failing the children as well. The parents are not the only one, neither are the foster parents even though this is what we have been accused of sometimes. Its like with anything else—all parents are not bad parents—all foster parents are not bad foster parents and all caseworkers are not bad caseworkers. What you have to do is figure out how to help everyone. And the chances of that happening are next to none. The systems greed for money has blinded them so that they cannot see the need for foster parents for our children and without money no one wants to be a foster parent. Won't you reach out and help the children by helping the foster parents. The children are in need of homes and without money there just will not ever be enough foster parents.—just remember that no one is perfect not even foster parents—and when you have someone to step in and try to be a parent to children that are not theirs and children that don't even like them, and they can take that child and turn him into a respectable child, a child that can deal with the hand that has been dealt him, a child that was torn up on the inside, a child that could never look at people the same, a child that went from failing grades to honor roll, a child that had nightmares to sleeping well at night, a child that thought everybody hated him to a child that could except rejection, a child that wet the bed for whatever reason and he stopped and not because of the pills he was being given for wetting the bed, a child that has never been to church to a child that loves church—foster parents account for 90% of that change—not therapy, not caseworkers, not pills—foster parents. And yes, please don't misunderstand there are foster parents that are just not good for kids either. I mentioned this before. How can you tell? Well the month that the caseworker didn't visit could have been the month the child wanted to tell them something. Maybe if you were not so concerned about training hours and writing people up for petty things you would have taken time and talked more and maybe you would have been able to tell something was wrong instead of looking for error in paperwork all the time. Maybe if you took the time to take the child to get a coke every now and then maybe even fake like you care he may feel comfortable talking to you and would of told you that something was wrong. Maybe if for his birthday you sent him a gift—just simple things that make a child feel comfortable about talking. You could just send out the card because you care, they are 2 for a $1 at the dollar store—that's not too expensive. You don't even have to drill him like you do as if to put things in his mouth—once the idea is planted he is going to run with it and you are to. I don't know but if you are going to constantly ride everybody else someone need to ride you as well. None the less and even with the cases of bad foster parents I still have to say foster parents I applaud you, I applaud us. I pray for you, I pray for us, I pray for the system. The children need us, we have to fight to make it better, and I appreciate the work we do. We sometimes have bad days I think about that even if no one else ever does. I am sorry for the foster parents that hurt children—I am sorry for the parents that hurt children—I am sorry for the system that is failing our children and if by chance you are an agency and none of these things pertain to you, I take my hat off to you. We thank God for you and we need to know who you are. People will always follow the best help. They will always go where they are appreciated most. These are not complaints, this is the way it is, and this is the way foster parents feel. Look at secretaries—even they have a day designated to them. With all that foster parents do—and with the big difference that we make—why is there not a day set aside for us? Why is there not a day designated for the children? Maybe they could go and get a free ice cream cone—a free candy bar—and its not designed to make them feel like they are better than anyone else its just to help them to see that they are special too. We really thank God for our families—and for the love and the gifts on our special days. Thank God for the churches that prays for us and gives us gifts. Thank the many people that pray for us. When it comes to foster children—we as parents would like for them to know that we have a job to do and it's not just a job. We really really care and want you to not feel like you are just another kid because you're not. We know that it's hard, it has to be. No, we haven't been in your position at least some of us haven't but, we try to understand. We're not trying to replace anyone, in your life, we can't. Yes we would like for you to care about us a little bit at least. After all, we do all that we can and are allowed to do. So bear with us please, we're not perfect and we can admit that we're not. Allow us to make mistakes and when we make them know that we are trying and will try to do better. If you would just try to hang in here and never feel like you are just a kid because you're not, you are a very special kid and that mean a lot.

To foster children all over the world—never ever feel like you are alone—never ever feel like you are different—you're not—please never feel like you're not loved—you are—hold your head up and stick your chest out. It doesn't matter where you are or who you're with, just remember regardless of what anybody say—.you are loved. It doesn't matter what other children say, how bad people may try to make you feel. Be the best that you can be. You are special and you are somebody.

Foster parents hang in there, no matter what. You are special as well. No foster child could make it without the foster parent, be it in a home setting or a facility. When it get almost too hard to bear you know who to call and he will supply you with the strength you need to go that extra mile. Sometimes it get hard it seem because you have a lot of people talking and not doing anything but criticizing. And you know you are doing the very best that you can. When you know you are right stand tall and don't take down—you have the right to state your opinion, to state your case. You have the right to be in disagreement with the system. You can speak—you have that right too. And it should not threaten your license. They have legal measures that you can take when being mistreated and accused of doing things that you as a foster parent know that you didn't do. Don't just settle for anything. You don't have to. We do have someone in our corner.

To those of you that have never had the opportunity to work with, take care of, live with, or even be in the presence of a foster child. They cannot help that fact. Pray for them, help them—and even for children that have never been in that position, be thankful and hope you never do. God Bless

I have also added a few letters that were inserted by people that are not foster parents and don't care to be. They just wanted it to be known that they do play a part in this situation also. We are hoping for the best and also hoping that things will change for the better of the children as well as the foster parent. If people can look past their own needs and think about the children it would not be hard to give foster parents what they deserve, whatever it may be. The need for foster parents is not going to go down no time soon or later. We have more and more children. Children are not only being taken away from parents they are also being taken away from foster parents. We have to make sure that our children feel safe and loved, they cannot do it themselves. It's so wonderful when you have to reach out for someone and that someone is there, in reaching distance. Everyone can't throw in the towel someone has to stand. There is enough love to go around sometimes you just don't realize that you have that much love to give. Giving it is so hard to do for some people and even giving of themselves. Yes, it's stressful sometimes and no it's not for everyone but it is for someone. When you look at these children the average person fail to realize that many children that have been in foster care are adults now. They've gone on with their lives and they didn't give up they did well. They made the best of a bad situation and whether they got past the hurt or not, they did not fail. They are a success. They are a success because they chose to be—they made good choices. Maybe as time change the system will be able to maybe build facilities large enough similar to dormitories and colleges. These facilities would house the children in a whole different setting and there would not be a need for as many foster parents. If there was a need there would be people available. It would also be a safer place for the children to be if monitored correctly. Therapist, dentist, and everyone that is needed would be on the premises. That would save millions of dollars. This way siblings would not have to be separated—adopted out, when there are no homes for these children they could live at this facility. That's just a thought, I don't really know if that would even work but it would be nice if it could.

The facility would be more like a home and not a RTC or a shelter. Big difference. Me personally, I will always think and hope for something better for the children. Your imagination could really run away with you if you let it. Just think even the schools could be on the grounds—how convenient.

I hope that I have somehow made a difference. These thoughts are out here now—I think I have said what so many foster parents wanted to say but did not want to deal with the consequences. I know that some of these concerns touched people in many areas—no offense just truth from my point of view. I know you have yours and you are entitled. Yes, I am going to always work with children. 15 years of day care, 8 of foster care—I can't stop now.

To the readers of this book:

I just wanted to comment on the parents. I think that parents of these children should be ashamed. Why can't you take care of your own children? It may get hard sometimes but, you can make it. I know you can don't you know that your children love you and want no one except you? No one can take your place, they have a special place in their hearts for you and only you—all children do. I am going to pray that all parents step up to the plate and make a difference in their children's life—God Bless

Muleshoe, Texas

To the Foster Parents:

You are doing something I would never do. But I pray for you all the time. I know it's not the children's fault but it's a lot of work. The system doesn't want to pay you for doing it. Whoever is running the system need to be put in check? I will continue to hope and pray for a change. Thank you

Lubbock, Texas

Dear Reader:

Foster parents make a very huge difference in the world when it comes to children. Why the system doesn't want to pay them is beyond me. It has to be a tremendous amount of work and since the foster parent seem to do the largest portion—shouldn't they be compensated for it?

West Texas

To the children that read this book—
We Love You

Dallas, Texas

Author—

I think you did a wonderful job on this book. I also want to say that even if you don't make a difference—you really tried and that's better than some people did. If ever anything come up about this I want to make sure that I give my input—I love you for being a foster parent.

Levelland, Texas

To the ones in charge:

I just want to applaud you for at least trying. You make a difference as well, but you get your special days. You should try not to be so hard on foster parents and take into consideration the work that they do. I also agree that there should be a special day set aside for foster parents and foster children. It's like neither of them is important. When she said that the secretaries have a day that's true. So why shouldn't they? I will bet you never thought about it did you?

Lubbock, Texas

To the author:

Thanks for this book

Austin, Texas

These are only a few of the letters and input that I received. I tried to pick one or two of each. I am surprised at the people that agreed to participate when asked. There are many people that have things to say and they also have concerns. I guess until now they just didn't get involved. I am hoping that as we go forward and try to make a larger difference in the lives of these children that the world will join in and work hard to make a difference also. We have to take care of our children. I cannot stress enough the importance of keeping our children safe and making them feels safe. No worries until its time. At least allow them the opportunity to be a happy child. I want to thank everyone that purchased this book and I am hoping that it will help you have a better look at the inside so that you won't have to be on the outside looking in. I also know that everyone don't agree with the book and that's o.k. The saying if the shoe fit wear it and if it don't take it off—simply means that if the information pertains to you then fine—if it don't then don't worry about it. This is in no way aimed at any one individual but us as a whole—the purpose being so that prayerfully there will be a change made for the better. I chose this particular cover because it cover so many emotions that everyone go through at one time or another when you are dealing with stressful situations. It doesn't matter who you are adult or child. Children in care go through so many things so I hope that the words on this cover will take care of most of them if not all of them.

Even though so much mentioned in this book has to do with money, its speaking on mainly compensation. A little on greed when it come to money. There is a difference in the two.

Last but not least a poem from me.

THE TEARS THAT LINGER

It all happened one day, no warning came
All the feelings were introduced and knew no name
The name did not matter for with each child it was the same
The heaviness, the confusion, and so, so much pain

The tears they linger, trying not to fall
I wipe and wipe my face only to find that that's not all
As I try to stand straight, chest out, standing tall
Please help me to break through this resistant wall

Sometimes emotions can be a confusing ball
And at some time or another enter the hearts of all
As I struggle to break through this great resistant wall
Help me to get past the tears that linger and will not fall

MARY WEBB